CHERISHED THREADS

"Woven with memories, sealed in letters, and cherished with love."

SUNIL KUMAR MAGATAPALLI

A Book By:
FOREVER SHININGS
Instagram - @forevershinings.co
forevershinings1@gmail.com

Book Title: Cherished Threads

Book Author: Sunil Kumar Magatapalli

Published By: FOREVER SHININGS

First Edition: 2025

ISBN: 978-93-5605-575-9

With The Blessings Of

Shirdi Sai Baba

NOTE FROM THE AUTHOR

Dear Reader,

This book isn't just fiction—it's a thread of emotions, stitched with memories and moments that shaped me.

I've often wondered how threads hold fabric together. Now I know: it's the same way memories hold us—gently, tightly, and sometimes, unexpectedly.

Some sisters write to us.
Some walk beside us.
Some arrive like silence, and leave like prayer.

But all of them shape us, and stay within us—forever.

This book is my humble tribute to every Akka, every Thangai, every Didi, every sister-friend,

Who stood like quiet strength in the background,
Whose care was felt more in moments than in words.

You are the smile behind these pages,
the strength between the lines,
and the reason this story found its voice.

This book is stitched with your love.
And for that—I bow with a full heart.

With love,
Sunil Kumar Magatapalli
(Yours, Sudheer)

INDEX

CHAPTER 1: SUMMER OF 1992

Some memories live in soft light — not the kind that blinds, but the kind that glows gently, like a diya flickering on Diwali night, or the early morning sun on childhood rooftops. That's where Sudheer kept his memories of her.

She wasn't just family. She was *Akka*. His cousin by relation, but his elder sister in every sense of the word that mattered. Her name was Kavitha — but to Sudheer, she had always been *Akka*.

In the early years, their families lived in the same town. During festivals, their houses would come alive with laughter, sweets, and noisy cousins chasing each other around. But no matter how many friends or relatives were around, Sudheer only wanted to be with her.

So much so, that even as a small boy, he would cry — just to go sit in *Akka*'s classroom. He didn't understand why he couldn't. All he knew was that he felt safest near her, happiest around her.

He would sit beside her during temple visits, hold her hand at family gatherings, and follow her like a shadow, soaking in her stories, her songs, her smile.

But in life, even the most beautiful moments are often brief.

In second standard, Sudheer's father moved to another town. The days of shared sweets, joint family dinners, and joyful moments with Akka faded into memory. The goodbyes weren't dramatic — just a quiet understanding that things were changing.

Still, life had a way of weaving them together once in a while. Akka would visit during a few holidays, and those rare moments became golden bookmarks in Sudheer's growing years. Short visits, but full of warmth — as if no time had passed.

Then came the *summer of 1992*.

Sudheer was in his teens by then, studying in Plus Two. He had been away for a while, in another town, undergoing treatment. It was a difficult phase — physically exhausting, emotionally tender. But summer holidays brought hope. Rest. A return to the familiar, but fate had other plans again.

Akka and her family had come to visit. She had been in *his house*, laughing with his parents, maybe even sitting in the room where he used to read. But the day Sudheer returned from treatment, she had already left.

Gone. By mere hours.

"There was no way to inform them," his mother said, quietly. "We had no phone, and they had to leave early." Sudheer sat in silence, the weight of that moment pressing into his chest. He stared at the place where she might have sat. Listened for echoes that were no longer there.

And something shifted inside him that day — something soft, something aching.

That missed meeting in 1992 became the turning point. Because sometimes, it takes distance — or a near miss — to realize how deep a bond truly runs.

A few weeks later, the first letter arrived.

It was in her familiar handwriting. Neat, slightly slanted letters that seemed to smile off the page. His heart skipped. His hands trembled.

He opened it slowly, carefully, like it was something sacred.

The letter began in her comforting voice — warm, affectionate, as if she was sitting right in front of him.

"Sudheer… I heard from Amma that you had just returned. I felt so bad when I came to know we missed each other. I was looking forward to seeing you too. It's been so long since we spoke properly. But don't worry... Next year again we will meet. I promise. Until then, you write to me. Okay? Tell me everything.

How are your studies? Is your leg better now? I'm waiting to hear from you.

With lots of love, Your *Akka.*"

He read the letter three times that night. Not because he didn't understand it the first time — but because he didn't want to stop feeling it.

Her words stitched something back together inside him. That soft voice in ink — full of concern, reassurance, and quiet strength — was all he needed.

And that was how it began.

It all began with a simple letter—but what followed was a stream of soul-touching exchanges between Sudheer and his *Kavitha Akka*. What started as casual sharing soon blossomed into a bond woven with melodies, memories, and heartfelt thoughts. Beyond everyday happenings, one major shared passion stood out: their undying love for Hindi films and songs.

Akka, always a step ahead in Odisha where Hindi films released earlier, would often write about watching *"Dil Hai Ke Maanta Nahin"* or other latest releases. Sudheer, back in Andhra, would read those words with glittering eyes and wait eagerly for the film to arrive at his local theatre. The thrill wasn't just in watching the film, but in knowing she had seen it too—like watching it together, apart.

Those were eventful days for Sudheer. He'd mentally calculate how many days it would take for his letter to reach Akka, and when hers might return. His home sat a little away from the main road, but that never stopped him from walking up to the gate and gazing down the lane—hoping to catch a glimpse of the postman. On days when a letter from Akka arrived, his joy knew no bounds. It was as if the world had handed him a slice of heaven.

In that delicate phase of his growing life, when the world seemed large and emotions deeper than words could say, a single letter from his Akka meant everything. It wasn't just paper and ink—it was connection, care, and the comfort of knowing someone, somewhere, truly understood.

A letter turned into a lifeline. One reply became two, then three, until the letters flowed like conversations across time and space — each envelope a bridge, each word a thread that tied them back to each other.

CHAPTER 2: 1993: THE SUMMER WHEN WORDS MET EYES AGAIN

The ink didn't dry after the first letter. It flowed like a river gently discovering its path. Sudheer and Akka — Kavitha — had found a new world in paper and postage, a sanctuary where they could talk without interruption, feel without hesitation.

But even as their letters became longer and closer, life moved on, pulling Sudheer into a difficult turn.

It was exam time. His crucial Plus Two finals. And he was struck down by jaundice.

Family members advised him to rest, to skip the exams — but something in Sudheer didn' t allow it. This was his final year, a turning point, and deep inside, he didn't want to let it go. With quiet determination, he moved to his maternal uncle's house, where he could be looked after while attempting the exams.

He wasn't alone. His uncle became his pillar, offering both medical care and encouragement. Every morning, Sudheer would push through weakness and fatigue, and appear for his papers — one after another — fighting a silent battle of mind and body.

And in the spaces between, his thoughts would drift. Back home, summer was approaching. He knew his Akka would be visiting again with her brother and sister. The thought gave him strength. Every dose of medicine, every tiring walk to the exam centre, carried one silent wish: *Let me get better in time to meet her.*

Holidays brought a brief distraction. Another uncle's family visited, and Sudheer joined with his cousins in laughter, long lunches and photo sessions. But his heart, quietly, was looking out the window, watching the road. Staying at his uncle's place in Visakhapatnam was always a pleasure. He liked his uncle a lot—mornings were spent with books and gentle advice on how studies could lead to a better future, while evenings were filled with joy—movies, beach visits, ice creams, and cousin fun. But that year, even with all the excitement, Sudheer felt restless. He knew Akka would be visiting home soon, and more than anything, he wanted to be there to welcome her. So, for the first time, he chose to return back early He waited. Counted the days.

And then, almost like a soft blessing, his health began to turn. Slowly but surely, he regained enough strength. And with that, he returned home —

He could sense it — a quiet flutter in his heart told him that Akka's visit was just around the corner. The air itself felt different, charged with a kind of excitement only a long-awaited reunion could bring.

That evening, while playing chess with cousins at their house, laughter echoing around him, he suddenly received the news: Akka had already arrived at his home.

Time stood still for a moment. His heart skipped a beat — or maybe several. He couldn't contain himself. Without even finishing the game, he grabbed his slippers and dashed out, barely noticing the familiar streets he raced through. A thousand smiles bloomed quietly within him, each one reflecting a memory, a letter, a moment they had shared.

As he neared the gate of his home, he slowed down, not out of exhaustion, but overwhelmed by anticipation. "How would she look now? Will she recognize the grown-up me at once?" he wondered. He gently pushed open the door, his eyes searching eagerly, his ears hoping to catch that beloved voice calling his name.

And there she was — standing in the hall, with the same affectionate smile, her eyes brimming with unshed emotion. The years melted in a heartbeat.

That moment — that first glimpse of Akka again after such longing — felt like a dream turning real.

After all the letters, after countless days of dreaming and nights spent staring at the ceiling, imagining that moment—it finally happened. Sudheer met his *Kavitha Akka* again, for the first time since their bond had bloomed through ink and paper.

As his eyes caught sight of her, standing there with that familiar, gentle smile and a caring spark in her gaze, something inside him stirred. She looked even more graceful than his memories could hold. When she softly asked, “How are you, Sudheer?”—with that concern only she could offer—he felt like a piece of heaven had landed right in front of him.

He had waited so long, imagined this reunion in so many ways—but reality was far warmer, richer, and more comforting than even his letters could have captured. At that moment, all the waiting, all the words exchanged in ink… had found their voice in her presence.

And from that day, it was as if time rewound to their childhood.

They spent soft, quiet evenings on the terrace. The moon would hang gently in the sky as Kavitha let Sudheer rest his head on her lap, gently stroking his hair as they spoke of dreams, fears, and nothing in particular. The breeze carried the scent of mango blossoms and shared secrets.
Then came a family wedding at cousins’ house. The house overflowed with relatives, cousins, food, and festivities. But for Sudheer, the world still narrowed to Akka. Whether in a crowd or a quiet room, his eyes would seek her, his voice would soften when she was near.

Amid this joy, one shadow lingered — his exam results. He had written them in the middle of illness. Doubts crept in.

But Akka, ever his anchor, smiled and reassured him in her usual warm way. "You've already won, Sudheer. You didn't give up. The results will only prove what I already know."

And she was right. The results came — and Sudheer had passed well.

There was celebration at home. His parents were proud, but Sudheer found his joy in simpler things: VCR movies with cousins, long hours of indoor games — chess, ludo, scrabble — and walks to nearby theatres to watch films. One of the last memories from that summer was the studio photo. They had all dressed neatly and smiled, but somehow, the picture came out oddly serious. Later, they laughed endlessly at their solemn faces, teasing each other over who looked like they were scolded.

But all seasons must end.

The day came when Akka and her siblings had to leave. The house, once full of laughter, now echoed with silence. Sudheer stood at the gate long after they left.

He didn't speak much for a while.
But the letters returned.

This time, they grew deeper. Full of long paragraphs, shared stories, and the comfort only handwritten words can bring. Sudheer waited for the postman every day. Each time he walked past without stopping, Sudheer felt a hollow tug.

One day, when the postman hadn't arrived, his father returned from the shop holding an envelope.

Akka's letter had been delivered there. Sudheer opened it like treasure — and her handwriting, flowing with love and affection, soothed every inch of his heart.

Raksha Bandhan came. Akka had sent beautiful rakhis through post — but they got lost in transit. When they realized they were undelivered, both felt the weight of the miss.

In her next letter, she wrote:

"Sudheer... the rakhi may not have reached, but you are always tied to my heart. A thread can break, but this bond never will."

Alongside affection, they shared other joys too. Both loved Hindi songs — Binaca Geet Mala was a shared ritual. They would list out top rankings, discuss songs, They'd note down the weekly Top 10, and if one of them missed an episode, the other would make sure to include the updated list in the next letter. These weren't just rankings—they were cherished codes between two hearts. That connection carried through the year.

As Sudheer moved into graduation, life became busy with lectures, books, and new people. But Akka never drifted away. Their letters remained the quiet bridge between past and present.

And in every word written, in every envelope sealed, they continued to hold each other across time, space — and growing years.

CHAPTER 3: TWO SUMMERS, ONE HEARTBEAT

The summer of 1994 unfolded like the soft pages of a diary—filled with moments both tender and thrilling. Sudheer, now growing into adulthood, still held within him the childlike joy of reunion. This time, it was not Akka visiting his town. It was Sudheer making the journey.

He was accompanied by his younger brother and a brother-in-law, who joined midway through their journey. The train ride itself became a precious memory — a long-awaited escape. As the train chugged past stations, Sudheer sat by the window, carefully noting each one down in his diary. The familiar rhythm of the train, the smell of chai at stations, and the promise of meeting his Akka filled him with butterflies.

At the destination station, Sudheer's heart beat faster.

Waiting on the platform were Akka's younger sister, Anitha and their father. But instead of the expected embrace, they played a little prank:

"Akka? Oh… she's gone to her uncle's house," they said with mock seriousness.

Sudheer's face dropped, unable to hide his disappointment.

After he reached their home, then came the laughter — a familiar figure opened the door. His Akka. Smiling, arms open. That single moment of reunion washed away all the fatigue of travel.

Once again, the comfort of being in her presence made everything brighter. The routines resumed — laughter, meals, shared secrets, lazy hours — but it wasn't the activities that mattered. It was her. Her presence.

At night, they shared a bedroom, listening to soft, romantic melodies of the 90s. Kumar Sanu, Alka Yagnik, Udit Narayan sang the background score to their quiet conversations. Though both were loyal fans of the golden voices — Rafi, Lata, Kishore, and Mukesh — these newer songs from *Aashiqui*, *Saajan*, and others nestled into their hearts just as warmly.

Days passed in a gentle blur. They visited her friends, went for outings on bicycles, caught a movie, and were even taken to Akka's vast college campus — a place that seemed like another world to Sudheer.

Sudheer's brother had an exam in a nearby town, so he left with others. But Sudheer, still nursing his recovering leg, stayed behind. Akka could have gone too — but she didn't. She stayed.

That quiet gesture meant the world to him. She never said much. Just smiled. But in that smile, Sudheer read volumes. He was never alone when she was around.

Eventually, the first parting of the season came. A lump in his throat, tears he swallowed. Only consolation he found on that parting day -Anitha accompanied them back to his town, bringing along a continuation of the bond — and some sweet memories shared anew.

Though Sudheer's heart always beat a little louder for Kavitha Akka — his dearest, irreplaceable soul-sister — he held a quiet, affectionate place for her younger sister, Anitha, too. Anitha was also older than him, yet the bond they shared had its own distinct flavor — lighter, playful, yet deeply comforting.

Now as Anitha stayed at Sudheer's home, those moments carved a gentle space in his memory. Whether it was sharing mango slices during lazy afternoons, listening radio songs, or simply chatting and playing indoor games during power cuts, their time together was simple, but special.

Days later, Akka and her brother visited their town too — a second reunion in one summer. More smiles, more shared times, more warmth. But as always, time moved fast. The goodbyes returned, and so did the waiting.

The letters resumed, filling the silence in their absence. Then came an unexpected gift — a surprise visit by Akka alone for some work. Sudheer hadn't known. She just arrived.

In the world before smartphones, before instant messages, this kind of surprise felt like magic.

They met, talked, and for a few brief hours, all worries melted away. Her comforting words, the way she placed her hand on his head in blessing — Sudheer soaked in every second.

This visit became a cherished jewel in his memory. Proof that some bonds didn't need planning — they found their own time to bloom.

And so, even as time marched forward, even as studies and life crept in, the letters kept flowing. Because theirs was not just a relationship built on shared childhood — it was sustained by handwritten dreams, shared melodies, and hearts that never stopped waiting for the next moment together.

CHAPTER 4: THE NEARNESS AND THE SILENCE

The year 1995 began with a surprise that Sudheer could never have dreamt of — Akka and her family shifted to his very town, settling into a house just a few lanes away. It felt surreal. The one he once wrote letters to with longing was now within walking distance.

And they came back on a very special day — Sudheer's birthday, in June. It was the best gift he could've received. But what followed was unexpected — a quiet shift in their dynamic.

The handwritten letters, once soaked in emotions and pages long, slowly disappeared. The distance between them had vanished, but so had the ink and paper that once bridged their hearts. Now, they saw each other almost daily — quick hellos, shared moments, conversations at the gate or during casual visits.

Yet, each meeting also came with its own little parting. The yearning was different now — not for physical presence, but for the kind of emotional closeness that letters once delivered so effortlessly.

Raksha Bandhan came with all its joy. Akka and her sister prepared a delightful spread of homemade delicacies.

The ritual of tying rakhi was performed with love and laughter, and the camera clicked away to capture the memories.

They eagerly waited for the photos to develop — as people did in those days of film rolls and photo studios. But when the prints arrived, their hearts sank. The battery in the camera hadn't been properly installed. Every photo from that beautiful day was gone. Lost.

It felt like a quiet heartbreak. A celebration remembered only in their minds.

Still, life moved forward. They celebrated Anitha Akka's birthday with a trip to the cinema — a rare treat that made the day feel like a small festival. Anitha too had joined a local college to continue her graduation which made their families feel more closely knit than ever.

But while smiles and greetings continued, something was missing. Something only Sudheer could sense — that lingering space where handwritten words used to live.

Akka was still there — and yet, sometimes it felt like she was already beginning to drift into a new chapter of her own. One that would take her further away. But for now, Sudheer held on to the small moments. The daily smiles. The glances that said what words no longer did.

And unknowingly, they were both walking toward a future that would change everything.

CHAPTER 5: THE SUMMER OF GOODBYES AND BEGINNINGS

The summer of 1996 was painted in shades of change — bittersweet, quiet, and unforgettable.

Sudheer was in the final stretch of his degree. While preparing for his last exams, there was also a collective national hope in the air — India's dream run in the Cricket World Cup. Like millions of others, he and his friends waited with bated breath for that magical win. But the heartbreak came swiftly — India lost in the semifinals. The defeat lingered in the air, dampening spirits just days before his final exams.

Still, life moved on. He picked up his pen and marched into the exam halls, his heart still heavy but determined. Outside the academic world, his heart was quietly counting down another timeline — Akka's wedding, just a few days after his exams.

The joy for her new journey was sincere. Sudheer celebrated her happiness, smiled through every ritual and every blessing shared. But deep within, a silence took root. One that comes only when you know you're about to lose something irreplaceable.

Her marriage came and went in a beautiful blur. When she left for her new home, she bent down and kissed his forehead — a blessing, a farewell, a silent promise that nothing would change.

The rest of the family headed to her in-laws' place for the reception. Sudheer stayed behind, assuming the moment had passed.

But it hadn't.

Just as he felt the weight of missing her, Akka's father returned. "Come with me," he said, gently. In that moment, Sudheer's heart leapt.

At her new home, built upon the terrace of an old house, he found something magical. A room filled with fresh paint, soft curtains, sunlight — and Akka. Her world had changed, but her warmth remained untouched.

He returned home eventually, holding on to the scent and light of that new place — a heaven on the terrace.

The results of his exams came soon after — he had passed.

Now began a new phase — the search for a job, trips to his uncle's place, the process of collecting documents. It was his uncle who helped him arrange for the medical exemption certificate he needed to claim a government job through the Staff Selection Commission, whose exam he had already cleared the year before.

When he returned home after all the formalities, another beautiful surprise waited. Akka was in town.

Another few days of togetherness — movie outings, dinners at small hotels, long talks about life and the future. She lifted his spirits once again, like she always did. He told her about his exam results, his dreams, his doubts. And she listened.

Then came yet another parting. But this time, it felt more permanent.

Sudheer returned to his routine. But now, he waited for the postman with a new kind of hope — not only for Akka's letters, but for his posting order too.

And then, one day, the letter came.

His appointment order. His job.

In that moment of joy, his thoughts flew to Akka. And the pen once again touched paper. The letters resumed — perhaps slower, more infrequent, but filled with the same love and connection.

Akka was now living in a different world, with new responsibilities. Replies came late, sometimes not at all. But that was okay. Because the bond remained.

And thus, 1996 came to a quiet close — a year of partings, of exams passed and worlds changed, of a boy becoming a man, holding on to the light that was his Akka.

CHAPTER 6: A CITY OF MEMORIES, A HOME OF NEW BONDS

Sudheer's first posting felt like a quiet miracle — a return to the roots of his being. The city of Visakhapatnam, with its golden beaches and blue-tinged horizon, welcomed him not just as a worker, but as a child of its soil. It was here that he had once taken his first steps, where summer holidays were once painted with the laughter of cousins and the scent of mangoes.

Living with his uncle, aunt, and beloved grandmother in that familiar yet new world, Sudheer found something he didn't expect — a sister-like warmth in his uncle's wife. She wasn't just an aunt; she was a friend, a listener, a gentle soul who understood the emotional tides that surged quietly within him. He often spoke to her about his new office, colleagues, Akka — the bond, the letters etc.

The office life in Vizag moved steadily. Weekdays brought busy hours, laughter with colleagues, and long walks through the city's coastal charm. But the weekends… oh, the weekends were poetic. There were no mobile phones buzzing, no urgent pings or emails to answer.

Just the rhythm of time passing gently — books bought from roadside stalls, movies watched in single-screen theatres, the hush of a beach evening settling into his bones like peace.

One such weekend, fate played another little trick. Akka came visiting her relatives in the city — and Sudheer, out on a small outing, missed her arrival. The weight of another near-miss pressed on him. But this time, he wasn't willing to surrender to fate so easily.

In the thick of an unexpected rain, umbrella in hand, he rushed to a nearby STD booth — those old yellow cabins that held a thousand whispered memories. A quick call, a scribbled number, and soon, he was walking through the wet streets to find her. When he finally knocked and saw her open the door — surprise in her eyes, joy in her voice — he knew he'd reclaimed yet another memory. Technology may have been absent, but hearts still knew how to find each other.

Back at his uncle's home, Sudheer continued to find quiet joys — playing with his two-year-old nephew, receiving rakhis from the affectionate neighbour sisters, and quietly journaling the gentle rhythms of life. One of those neighbour girls, the eldest, became another sister in his emotional tapestry — until, one day, her own marriage pulled her away too. Another goodbye, another thread tugged from the heart.

Six years passed like a dream. Eventually, Sudheer's request for a transfer to his hometown was approved. What should have been a happy homecoming brought a deep ache — leaving behind his aunt, who had unknowingly become his sister like. Her parting blessings, gentle and warm, reminded him of the kiss Akka had placed on his forehead on her wedding day. History, it seemed, had a way of folding back onto itself.

CHAPTER 7: A DREAM, A JOURNEY, AND A BEAUTIFUL MEMORY

Back in his hometown, life settled into a smaller office, a quieter rhythm. Letter writing with Akka continued — less frequent now, more grown-up perhaps, but no less sincere. The thread never truly snapped.

It was the calm before the storm —just months before his younger sister's marriage, Sudheer experienced one of the most exhilarating moments of his life. After clearing a few preliminary rounds over the phone, he received the news that he had been selected to participate in *Kaun Banega Crorepati*. The announcement sent ripples of excitement through his home, but for Sudheer, something even more thrilling awaited: his first-ever flight.

His uncle, a constant pillar of support, accompanied him on this adventure. Both of them were flying for the first time, and every moment felt grand and unforgettable — the buzz of the airport, the surreal experience of being airborne, and the growing realization that they were heading to Mumbai. For Sudheer, it wasn't just about a game show; it was about stepping into a new chapter of life.

The stay at a star hotel only added to the dreamlike atmosphere. It all felt almost too good to be true.

When the final shoot day arrived, Sudheer was filled with awe.

Before the final shoot, Sudheer had gone through several preliminary practice rounds. During these sessions, he consistently answered questions correctly but often fell short when it came to speed. The competition demanded not only accuracy but also quick reflex In the final episode shoot, Sudheer got only one opportunity to secure a place in the coveted hot seat. This chance required him to answer both correctly and faster than the other contestants. Though he answered the question correctly, he wasn't fast enough to claim the spot.

After this, the remaining contestants moved on to the Fastest Finger First contest — a separate round where the winner was determined by who scored the highest points and, if tied, who answered the fastest. Sudheer performed steadily, and when the final scores were announced, he had just one point more than the second-highest scorers. Because of this slight lead in points, the tie-breaker based on speed was not needed.

This narrow victory in the Fastest Finger First contest won him a prize of ₹2 lakhs — a moment of triumph that Sudheer would cherish forever, made all the more special by the dreamlike experience of staying at a star hotel and participating in the grand event.

But what etched the experience into his soul was a last-minute handshake with none other than Amitabh Bachchan Ji...

It was brief, but in that fleeting second, time seemed to stand still. The couple of photos taken with the legendary actor along with his uncle would remain among Sudheer's most cherished possessions — tangible proof of a dream touched, if not fully lived.

That journey didn't just bring excitement; it marked a turning point in Sudheer's life. It was a glowing memory forged just before the winds of change swept in. His sister's wedding was drawing near, and with it, the comfort of the familiar would give way to a new, evolving world.

And then came 2006. His own younger sister, the one he'd grown up with, the one who hadn't written letters but had shared whispers and secrets, also left home as a bride. As she walked into her new world, Sudheer felt the familiar emptiness return. The quietness of the house echoed in the chambers of his heart.

Once again, a sister had gone. Once again, he found himself staring at the sky, hoping that love — no matter where it resided — would always write back.

But life, in its quiet wisdom, knows how to mend even the softest cracks.

After his younger sister's marriage, Sudheer and his brother discovered something unexpected — a gentle bond with their new brother-in-law. He wasn't just a new addition to the family; he was someone they could laugh with, talk to, and feel at ease around.

Slowly, he became a friend — a bridge that helped them adjust to the space their sister once filled. Through shared jokes, late-night chats, and quiet understanding, this new connection offered comfort in its own way.

Some bonds are born of blood, others of fate — but all of them leave their mark.

CHAPTER 8: GRACE AMIDST STORMS - 2007-2008

The year 2007 brought a warm breeze into Sudheer's life when his younger brother Kiran got married. His wife, Ananya, entered their family with the grace of someone born to belong. Her presence transformed their home—every visit felt festive. She would prepare delicious dishes, engage warmly with every family member, and most importantly, treat Sudheer's parents with the love and care of a daughter.

Sudheer observed her quietly and fondly. Ananya carried a quiet dignity, a steady warmth that reminded him of the kind-hearted women he had always admired. Her laughter softened silences, and her thoughtful gestures made everyone feel seen. For Sudheer, she was not just a new family member—she was a calming presence that wove itself gently into their lives.

But joy, as life often reminds us, walks hand in hand with sorrow. In 2008, Sudheer's other younger brother, Raghav—with whom he shared not only a childhood but also a rare congenital health condition—was diagnosed with worsening kidney complications.

That year turned heavy. The family shifted into a space of worry, hospital corridors, quiet prayers, and countless moments of emotional strain.

Through it all, Kiran and Ananya, though just newly married, stood like unwavering pillars. They shouldered the responsibilities of caregiving with immense maturity—accompanying Raghav to hospitals, handling medications, and offering comfort and strength to the entire family.

Sudheer watched Ananya with deep respect. For someone so new to the family, she bore the weight of its sorrow with grace that was beyond her years. She remained calm, patient, and endlessly giving—supporting her husband, caring for her in-laws, and doing everything with a quiet, selfless love.

Yet, despite all the efforts and prayers, fate dealt its cruellest blow—Raghav passed away. The loss shattered the family. For their parents, it was a grief too vast to be expressed. For Sudheer, it was the heartbreak of losing a brother who had been more than a sibling—he had been a part of his own being, a silent partner in health battles, and a soul-twin in many ways.

Amidst the grieving days, a faint light appeared—Ananya was expecting. The news brought a pause in their mourning, a moment to lift their heads toward hope. Sudheer, though still aching inside, offered a silent prayer of thanks. In that moment, he saw the hand of the divine—easing one sorrow with the promise of a new joy.

Months later, a beautiful baby girl was born—delicate, radiant, and full of the kind of life the family had almost forgotten. Her tiny cries filled the silent halls. Her smile softened the grief still sitting in their hearts.

She became more than a child. She became a symbol of healing. A reminder that even after the harshest winters, spring finds its way back.

CHAPTER 9: BROKEN, YET BLESSED

It was a normal day in 2012,
Sudheer, working peacefully in his hometown, noticed a troubling infection near his ankle — something that refused to heal.

With a congenital defect shadowing him since birth, he was no stranger to medical worries. Yet this time, it felt different... heavier.

An initial surgery and debridement were done, but the infection stubbornly stayed.

Concerned, his uncle consulted specialists once again.

Their verdict came like a hammer blow — "**Below-knee amputation** would be the best and most permanent solution."

Sudheer couldn't believe it.

He was taken to a specialty hospital in Coimbatore, his brother & uncle by his side.

Even there, the experts repeated the same advice.

At first, Sudheer refused.

"What if I can't walk again?"
"What if life never feels normal again?"

That night, in the hospital bed, Sudheer lay awake, his mind a whirlwind of fears.

He thought of his aging parents, alone in their hometown, depending silently on their son.
He thought of his own solitary life, now shadowed by an uncertain future.

"How will I take care of them?"
"How will I take care of myself?"

But the doctors counselled him patiently, explaining the greater danger of untreated infection — and the shrinking chances of survival without intervention.

Broken inside, Sudheer agreed.

Sometimes, acceptance is the hardest battle.

The Operation and Aftermath

A few days later, the operation took place.

The bitter truth had to be swallowed — his leg was amputated below the knee.

In the hospital for almost a month, he faced some of his darkest days.

His uncle, his brother — their quiet support became his pillars.

His younger sister and brother-in-law also arrived, wrapping him with moral courage he didn't know he still had.

Sudheer tried to be brave, but the ache inside him went deeper than the missing limb.

When his little four-year-old niece saw him, her innocent sadness pierced his heart.

Even his aged parents, struggling with travel, came to be with him.

Their presence made his heart heavy and light at the same time.

Above all, his brother's wife — his sister-in-law, Ananya became a blessing.

Her care, her laughter, her delicious dishes filling the home with warmth — all these became the medicine no doctor could prescribe.

In her, Sudheer found not just a caretaker, but something precious he thought he lost —

He found another sister, a bond which he always cherishes...

Someone who soothed his broken spirit when he doubted himself the most.

The New Beginning

Days turned into weeks.

Wounds began to heal.

Pain faded into acceptance.

And then came the day Sudheer stood again a prosthetic leg supporting him, trembling but determined.

Exactly three months after the surgery, just as the doctors had promised, Sudheer took his first steps.

They were small, slow, unsure but they were his steps.

His *victory*.

A wave of humility flooded him.

He bowed his head silently, grateful to God for blessing him with a loving family thousand prayers of his mum and dad, which always stood like rock solid support..a uncle who's always with him through every thick and thin ever since his childhood..
a brother who stood as his shadow,
a sister-in-law who fed his heart with care,
a sister & brother-in-law who were there for him….
an Akka who worried from afar,

and the brilliant doctors, nurses, and prosthetists
who stitched not just his body, but his spirit back together.

Sudheer also felt an ocean of gratitude for the advancements in prosthetic technology, which gifted him the simple yet priceless miracle — the ability to *walk* again.

To *live* again.
To *dream* again.
He was still Sudheer.
A little changed outside,
but stronger, humbler,
and infinitely richer inside.

Months passed since Sudheer's operation, and the quiet struggle he endured slowly turned into an unspoken strength. His body, though still recovering, had found its rhythm again. He began to move forward, one careful step at a time, with his prosthetic leg firmly on the ground. Life, though altered, felt steady once more.

After the amputation, when Sudheer was finally fitted with a prosthetic leg, he felt a quiet closure to the Coimbatore chapter—a place etched in his memory for the sudden turn of events, the haunting surgery, and the emotional scars that lingered. He thought he had left that part of the story behind. But life, with its uncanny grace, had other plans.

In an unexpected twist, within a short span, his younger brother Kiran was transferred to Coimbatore. The family moved there, and not long after, a new chapter unfolded—a beautiful baby boy was born the following year, right in the very city that had once held only pain in Sudheer's mind.

It felt like life, or perhaps something higher, was gently stitching joy into the cracks of old wounds. Just as the family had once received the news of Ananya's first pregnancy soon after Raghav's passing, here too, a soft miracle had arrived to ease a past sorrow.

Sudheer often looked back at that turn of events with quiet awe—how Coimbatore, once a symbol of fear and loss, now held laughter, new beginnings, and the echo of a baby's first cry. It felt like a divine reassurance—that even in the places we fear to revisit, life plants seeds of healing, if only we choose to see them.

In the weeks following Sudheer's amputation, when his world had slowed into a rhythm of recovery and reflection, three more visitors came to see him—each one gently opening a window to a part of his past that still lived quietly within him.

The first was his dearest Kavitha Akka—the one who had once shaped his thoughts through handwritten letters and taught him the power of expression, emotion, and sibling love. Her presence felt like a piece of his inner world had stepped out into the open.

With just a few words and a long, quiet look, she reminded him of how deeply their bond ran—untouched by time or distance.

The second was Meena, his childhood sister— Her home had stood just next to the little card shop where Sudheer used to frequent, especially during those special days when he picked out greeting cards with long, emotional messages for Kavitha Akka. Every visit to that shop turned into a memory with Meena—playful teasing, shared snacks, and laughter that echoed louder than the town around them. Their bond was spontaneous and pure, filled with the kind of joy only childhood can hold. Seeing her again after so long, in a moment when he needed grounding, felt like time had reached back to hug him.

The third visitor was from a different part of life—Devika, a senior colleague from his VSP days, who had quietly become an elder-sister figure. Sudheer had long admired her grace under pressure, her calm strength, and the quiet way she led others. He fondly remembered his visits to her home — warm, filled with laughter, and wrapped in that intangible comfort called belonging. Though years had passed since they'd worked together, she appeared that day with the same quiet presence. She didn't speak much, but she didn't have to—her visit was a gesture of deep respect. In her eyes, Sudheer wasn't someone broken; he was someone remembered, valued, and still whole.

Those visits didn't change what had happened. But they softened its edges. They reminded Sudheer that even in moments of greatest stillness, life continued to send its messengers of comfort—some through blood, some through memory, and some through simple presence.

Not all bonds need footsteps. Some simply arrive... and stay.

The year had offered Sudheer many surprises—some painful, others quietly radiant.

And among the radiant ones was a bond born not in a hospital ward or childhood home, but on a screen.

It began with a message on LinkedIn.

Sudheer had read about her—Sahana Didi—an officer once part of the very department he worked in. She had left government service to corporate world with work on rural empowerment projects, and her ideas moved him deeply.

He wrote to her. She replied.

What followed was not dramatic—no long phone calls or frequent chats. But there was a rhythm.

A Pongal wish here, a Diwali greeting there. A gentle encouragement during his recovery phase. A few articles shared. A few thoughts exchanged.

And in that soft digital corner, Sudheer felt something beautiful take root.

He called her *Didi*.

To many, it may seem ordinary—a LinkedIn contact turned kind acquaintance.

But to Sudheer, who had always found meaning in emotion over frequency, she was a sister whose presence didn't need proximity.

Though they never met, her words often arrived like the breeze before a storm—calming, thoughtful, timely.
He once wrote in his journal:

"with every message she sends, she ties something deeper—a thread to the heart."

CHAPTER 10: WHEN HOPE HELD ON

Some moments arrive quietly, but they change everything. This was one of those.

Sudheer had seen many phases in life — laughter, loss, letters, longing — but nothing prepared him for the long, silent ache that shadowed his younger sister Meera's life after her marriage. A soft-spoken soul with eyes that smiled more than her lips, she began her journey into married life with dreams as bright as any young woman's. But as years passed and no child came, the silence grew louder.

Thirteen years.

Thirteen years of waiting, trying, hoping.

Sudheer watched her fight this unseen battle — one that many couldn't even sense. Together, she and her husband tried everything: medical treatments — both modern and traditional — endless consultations, and quiet temple visits where they tied threads of faith onto trees and lit lamps against the wind.

Sudheer himself had taken her to doctors in his hometown, speaking to specialists, praying for a breakthrough. But fate had other plans.

In the middle of it all, his own life turned upside down — the leg pain, the hospital corridors, and eventually, the amputation. The world seemed to fall apart.

The treatments paused. Her hopes, already fragile, took another blow.

And yet — she endured. Patient, silent, unshaken. It humbled him.

Years passed. Even the most faithful among them began to quietly resign to fate. And then, one day, like a gentle breeze before a storm of joy, Sudheer's phone rang. It was her voice — trembling, almost uncertain.

"Anna… I'm carrying."

The world stopped.

His heart skipped a beat — then raced like it hadn't in years. Was this real? After thirteen winters of unanswered prayers, had God finally whispered "yes"?

Tears welled up in his eyes. He couldn't speak. He just let the silence wrap them both — a silence that said more than words ever could.

Sudheer's thoughts of gratitude also went to his uncle who prescribed alternative medication for his sister which might have fetched this much awaited moment and aunt who stood with her sister through this crucial phase giving moral support always.

But still fear crept at times. Her age, the risks, the complications — it all hung over their joy like a fragile curtain. Yet, they walked through it with faith, holding each other up with every scan, every test, every heartbeat heard through the machine.

She returned to Sudheer's home for the delivery few months before— a full circle moment that felt orchestrated by the divine. Even more beautifully, a childhood friend of Sudheer's, now a skilled doctor, was the one to care for her. Fate couldn't have written it better.

That year, Raksha Bandhan fell on Independence Day. As the morning sun lit up the sky, Sudheer was already awake, neatly dressed in his crisp uniform for flag hoisting. But it wasn't just the national pride swelling in his heart — it was something far more personal.

His sister, Meera, glowing with maternal grace and only days away from delivering her first child, had already begun the day with quiet joy. She tied the rakhi with a smile that reached her eyes, performed the aarti with steady hands, and offered him sweets with a love that had deepened over the years. It was a simple moment, yet it etched itself deep into Sudheer's memory.

What made that Raksha Bandhan so unforgettable was the beautiful confluence of emotions — a sister's affection, a brother's pride, the sacredness of the occasion, and the imminent arrival of new life that the whole family had prayed for.

As he stood quietly beside her, Sudheer's heart whispered a silent hope that— may she receive the choicest blessings from above, for the most divine moment of her life was about to unfold.

On that D -day at evening time, Sudheer paced the hospital corridor, hands folded, lips murmuring prayers. When the nurse finally stepped out and gently placed the newborn in his arms, he broke down.

A baby boy.

A soft, perfect miracle.

He looked at that tiny face and saw the answer to every silent night, every desperate prayer, every crushed hope. Tears streamed down his cheeks as he held his nephew close. This child wasn't just a baby — he was a promise kept.

The entire family rejoiced. His sister, glowing through her exhaustion after C-section, looked at her son like he was the only thing in the universe. Her husband, holding back sobs, stood beside her, overwhelmed. Sudheer's whole family joined and his niece and nephew were so thrilled to see the baby that arrived in their home…And Sudheer he just watched, his heart fuller than it had ever been.

In that moment, he felt something shift within him.

This wasn't just her happiness. It was his too. Every step of her struggle, he had walked beside her. Every disappointment, he had absorbed in silence. Seeing her complete — fulfilled as a mother — was a healing of his own wounds.

This child brought back something Sudheer had almost lost — faith in the impossible. Hope, no matter how buried, had bloomed.

And above all, it reminded him what love meant.

The love he had for his sister — it wasn't loud. It didn't always show. But it was fierce, unshakable, eternal. Watching her cradle her son, Sudheer felt something deeper than pride — it was pure joy, flowing from the very cent of his soul.

He had seen pain. He had lived through loss. But that day, holding that child, he felt something else — completion. Because when a sister finally becomes a mother after thirteen long years, it's not just her dream that comes true. It's her brother's too.

...a full circle moment that felt orchestrated by the divine. And what made it even more special was the presence of someone very dear to Sudheer — his childhood friend, now a doctor, who stepped in to care for his sister during the most crucial time.

She wasn't just a doctor in that moment — she was family. She knew the depth of the journey, the pain they had carried for years, and the magnitude of what this birth meant to Sudheer and his family.

After the successful delivery, as Sudheer held the newborn with trembling joy, he turned to her — eyes misty, heart full — and said, "I don't have words. Thank you for being a part of this… for making this miracle possible."

She smiled gently, eyes soft with emotion, and simply replied,
"Most welcome… and I feel very happy as I am part of your happiness."

Those words stayed with him. Because they weren't just a reply — they were a blessing.

Sudheer felt immense gratitude for her — not just as a doctor, but as a friend who walked into a defining moment of his life and left behind a permanent mark of love, care, and shared joy.

CHAPTER 11: THE THREAD THAT BINDS HEARTS

It was Raksha Bandhan, 2021.

And after many years, the house felt alive in a way Sudheer had almost forgotten.

For the first time in what seemed like ages, all three siblings were home—Sudheer, his younger brother Kiran, and their youngest sister, Meera. The rooms that once echoed with childhood chaos were now filled with grown-up voices, laughter, and the quiet comfort of belonging.
Their bond wasn't built on written letters or dramatic moments. It had blossomed naturally—born from shared childhood memories, school days, silly fights, and an unspoken loyalty that only siblings understand. It was a bond that matured quietly but deeply over time.

Meera, though the youngest, carried the warmth of a sister who had always observed more than she expressed. Sudheer had never found the right words to tell her how much she meant to him. But in his heart, in his quiet prayers, she was always present.

That morning, the house stirred with anticipation. Meera prepared the rakhi plate with traditional grace—tilak, ārati, rakhi, and sweets arranged carefully, just like their mother once taught her.

Sudheer's younger brother sat nearby, playfully guiding his own daughter and son through the rituals. It was a sight to cherish—two generations of Rakhi celebration woven together in one living room.

When Meera came forward to tie the rakhi on Sudheer's wrist, her gestures were calm and ceremonial. She applied tilak to his forehead, performed the āarati, tied the sacred thread with care, and fed him a sweet. There were no words—only a soft, sacred silence that spoke volumes.

Then, she turned to tie rakhi to their middle brother, her face lit with affection. Her two-year-old son watched everything with wide, wonder-filled eyes—absorbing a tradition too deep for words.

Their parents sat together, watching with quiet joy. For them, it was more than a festival—it was a full-circle moment. Their children, now parents themselves, carrying forward the very rituals they once led.

For Sudheer, this Rakhi was different.

His transfer orders had arrived. Soon, he would leave his hometown once again, and the house would return to its quieter self. But this celebration gave him something lasting—a moment of pure belonging, a memory sealed in the scent of kumkum, the glint of rakhi threads, and the sparkle in Meera's eyes.

That day, Raksha Bandhan wasn't just a ritual. It was a reunion.

A thread tied not only to the wrist—but to the heart, across time.

Sudheer always felt ……Rakhi holds together not just wrists… but memories, promises, and generations.

CHAPTER 12: THE MESSAGE THAT NEVER REACHED HER

There are joys in life that beg to be shared—not through announcements, but through a quiet glance, a smile, a few heartfelt words exchanged with someone who truly *matters*. Sudheer had such people in his life, and among them was one cousin sister, Meena—elder to him, graceful, and always gentle—whose house stood like a small oasis of warmth on the way to his greeting card shop visits.

She was never loud in her love, but her presence was always comforting. From childhood, Sudheer would drop by her house—sometimes for a few minutes, sometimes longer—and those moments were filled with an easy closeness. She'd ask how he was, offer something to eat, and never failed to send him back with a few loving words. She was part of that quiet support system Sudheer had built around himself—one of the few who really noticed things about him, even the ones he didn't say aloud.

Years passed. Life scattered people, shifted routines, and filled Sudheer's days with work, travel, and tension. After a particularly exhausting year in a difficult posting, Sudheer was finally transferred back to his hometown—a moment he had longed for. The relief was immense. He had come home.

He thought of her that day—how happy she'd be to hear the news. But amidst some other calls to family, and the rush of settling back in office, he forgot to message the good news. when he realized that, it was already late.

That moment never came.

Instead, what came was a message. A dreadful one.
She was gone.

A sudden heart attack had taken her away. The sister whose face he could still recall so clearly—the one who came to see him after his amputation, comforting him with her gentle laughter and quiet presence, the one he had hoped to surprise with his return back to hometown—had left without a goodbye.

Sudheer felt his world still.

In one night, the joy of returning home turned into a silence that would echo for months. He had wanted to see her smile and reply to the good news that he was back in home town, to share a few words that would've meant so much. But all he had left was the ache of knowing it was too late.

What broke him more was how she had just moved into a new home a month earlier, after a grand housewarming. Everything about her life had looked like a fresh beginning.

She had always been the one to ask Sudheer about his health, his struggles in far-off cities, how he was coping alone. Yet, not once had she mentioned her own health troubles. Not even a hint.

That was who she was—always caring, never complaining.

Festivals were never complete for Sudheer without messages for his loved ones, as he had a habit of sending midnight wishes for every occasion—New Year, Pongal, Diwali, Rakhi. And she, without fail, would respond with soft scolding and affection: "Why are you still awake, thambi? Please take care of your health."

Now, there was no reply.

Sudheer's birthday came just a few days after her passing. But this time, there was no celebration. He didn't want cake, candles, or messages. Instead, he walked to a small temple by a lake, one that reflected a peace he couldn't find anywhere else. He folded his hands, eyes closed, and whispered not a wish—but a prayer. To her.

"I'm home now, Akka. I made it back. I just wish you knew."

He stood there in silence, hoping that, wherever she was, she could feel the love that still poured out of him like a wound that wouldn't close.

Because Sudheer didn't just love his sisters. He lived for them. In every bond he formed—through letters, through festivals, through everyday acts of affection—he found meaning. He could never bear the idea of losing such a bond. But now he knew what it meant to lose a sister.

It meant losing a part of his childhood. A thread that tied him to the past. A gentle voice that reminded him to eat well, rest, and be strong.

Even today, as he sends out messages on festivals, his fingers pause. A part of him still expects her name to appear in the contacts list. His heart still wants to say, "Happy Anniversary," or "Take care, Akka." But he doesn't send them.

He sends them inward, into the quiet space of memory where she still lives.

And every time he thinks of her, he prays the same prayer: *May you be at peace, my Akka. You are missed more than words can hold.*

CHAPTER 13: WHEN SISTERS AND FRIENDS BECOME ONE

Sudheer had planned this visit to Brahmapur for a while. It wasn't just for the darshan of the local deity—though that was the heart of the trip—but also to spend time with his younger sister, who now lived in the same town. And above all, it was a chance to meet Kavitha, his dearest Akka who had always been more than just family—a guiding light, a comforting presence, someone who had quietly held his emotional world together through letters, calls, and memories.

But what made this visit truly special was a coincidence that had come to light a few years ago.

In a casual conversation on a WhatsApp group with his old college classmates, Sudheer had reconnected with a dear friend after many years. As they caught up, she mentioned that she was working as a teacher in a well-known school in the same town where Kavitha lived.

Without much thought, Sudheer responded,
"Oh, my cousin sister works in a school there too."
Curious, the friend asked for her name. When Sudheer replied, the reaction on the other side was one of pure astonishment.

"Wait—*Kavitha*? Your sister is Kavitha?! Arey Sudheer, she's my closest colleague and best friend! In fact, everyone at school calls us twin sisters!"

It was a moment of unexpected joy. Two important people from different stages of Sudheer's life were part of each other's world—and he had never known.

Though he had wanted to meet this friend again ever since, time and circumstances had always delayed the reunion. But not this time.

After completing his darshan and spending a peaceful afternoon with his younger sister, Sudheer made his way to Kavitha's house. She received him with her ever-familiar warmth—a mix of teasing affection and silent understanding. When he mentioned wanting to visit his old classmate—her "twin sister"—Kavitha laughed and said,
"Of course! Let's go together"

The visit that followed was nothing short of delightful. His friend welcomed them both warmly, and soon the three of them were reminiscing about college days, sharing updates from life, and reliving old laughter.

Kavitha and her friend teased each other like sisters. They shared stories of their time at school, each one revealing how deeply their bond had grown. For Sudheer, it was surreal—to see his childhood sister and college friend connected so naturally, as though life had quietly orchestrated it all.

The friend served gobi pakoda, Sudheer's favorite snack. Every bite felt like it carried the taste of nostalgia. They took selfies—laughing, posing, —and for that one evening, time melted.

As the evening came to a close, they took one last photograph together—a triangle of warmth, memory, and bond. And as Sudheer left, he carried more than images on his phone. He carried a sense of grace—of life bringing its own sweet surprises when least expected.

Some friendships evolve into family.
Some sisterhoods deepen through years.

And once in a while, both meet… over gobi pakoda, shared laughter, and timeless connection.

CHAPTER 14: DIYA IN SILENCE

After a long string of transfers, Sudheer found himself once again in Vizag—but this time, not in the warm shelter of relatives or the familiar bustle of childhood lanes. He had settled in a modest PG accommodation quiet corner in a rapidly changing city.

Work kept him busy during the day, but the evenings stretched into silence. The sea had always been more than scenery to Sudheer—it was solace. Now, living in a paying guest room opposite the beach in Vizag, his solitude found a rhythm.

The waves were like time itself—sometimes calm, sometimes restless, but always returning to the shore. It reminded him that no matter how much life pulled away, something within always found a way back. In those waters, Sudheer saw his own life—its crests of joy, its troughs of loss, and the persistent rhythm that kept it all moving.

On some evenings, with his back against the bench and eyes lost in the horizon, he'd hum softly—

"Zindagi kaisi hai paheli hai… kabhi toh hasaaye, kabhi yeh rulaaye…"

The tune echoed his thoughts — mysterious, unpredictable, yet still beautiful.

Under the moonlit sky, with salt in the air and music in his heart, Sudheer found comfort in the very uncertainty that once left him adrift.

He often spent his evenings by the shore, letting the breeze brush past him like an old friend. Later that night, Sudheer stepped onto the terrace, letting the cool breeze wrap around him like an old shawl. The full moon hung above, casting its soft glow over the rippling sea. Below, the waves whispered secrets to the shore.

He played a song close to his heart —

"Chaandni raat hai, tum mere saath hai..."

The lyrics flowed like the tide, stirring memories of bonds that still lived deep within him.

Though alone, he didn't feel empty. In that silver-lit silence, he felt the presence of those he loved — not beside him, but within him. The moon, the music, the sea — all bearing silent witness to a heart full of stories.

Sometimes, Sudheer would quietly read the old letters from his Akka. With mobiles and WhatsApp taking over, those handwritten notes became a lost charm. Yes, life became faster—but the joy of waiting, of holding a letter filled with love, was gone.

He often missed those magical days—when a letter from his Akka was a slice of heaven, when a new cassette of Rafi or Lata felt like treasure, when a random song on the radio made the day, and when a Sunday movie on Door darshan brought the whole family together. Those moments couldn't be replayed and maybe that's what made them so special.

Despite the loneliness, he stayed connected to sisters, now through WhatsApp chats and social media reactions. But even with constant digital presence, something felt missing—like a tune slightly off-key. In that vacuum stretch of life, he found a new acquaintance in Maya, a soft-spoken woman who lived in the neighbouring flat. Over the past few weeks, they'd struck a cordial bond—exchanging smiles, occasional conversations about food, books, and sometimes memories.

Two days later, he received a call. It was from Maya,

"Sudheer, can you come over in the evening?"
"Sure, Maya ji, everything okay?"
"Yes, yes… just come. No questions."

He was puzzled but agreed.

That evening, as he stepped into her house, the surprise took his breath away. Diyas flickered gently along the edge of the living room. A small thali with tilak, flowers, and sweets sat ready. The aroma of freshly cooked paneer curry and Halwa floated in the air.

"Happy Bhai Dooj, Sudheer," Maya said softly, her eyes gleaming.

Before he could react, she applied a tilak on his forehead, circled the aarti plate, and tied a red thread on his wrist.

"You told me you don't have anyone nearby to celebrate with. Today, I wanted you to feel remembered. You're like a brother to me now."

The warmth in her words mirrored memories from the past. He was reminded of all the sisterly bonds that shaped his soul.

Dinner was nothing short of a love letter in food:

- Roti with Paneer curry, thick and creamy—
- Pulihora, subtly tangy
- Gobi manchurian, crisp and spicy
- Halwa, so sweet and comforting

They sat across from each other, quietly eating, exchanging stories of siblings, festivals, and childhoods. As he left that evening, Maya handed him a small diary. "For your letters. The real kind. Start writing again, Sudheer."

That night, Sudheer sat by his window. The world outside buzzed with notifications, stories, and reels. But within, he had found something rare: a handwritten emotion, a real connection, a light in the silence.

That night, the Bhai Dooj diya burned steadily in the breeze, surrounded by stories unspoken. For Sudheer, the moment etched itself like a poem on his heart—quiet, intimate, and timeless. In Maya's gesture, he didn't just see a sisterly affection. He saw the echo of all the bonds he had ever cherished.

This bhai dooj celebration made Sudheer to rewind back to a glorious stretch of life way before he cherished much. It was from Kamala, sister-in-law by relation, but more truly a sister by affection. Her words were full of warmth, memory, and gentle advice She had once invited Sudheer to her home for Bhai Dooj, lovingly preparing his favorite dishes after secretly checking with his sister.

He remembered that day clearly—the lawn, the bougainvillea flowers, the smell of all his favourite dishes. In the lawn where gentle breeze greeted, they both engaged in a meaningful conversations about childhood memories, old Bollywood songs, and some routine job matters. Sudheer had always a token of highest regard of love n affection for Kamala which has developed over a period of time through candid conversations and chats. Though this one didn't involve writing letters, still he equally cherished this beautiful relationship which has blossomed out of mutual trust love and affection towards each other. Theirs was a relationship born not in ink, but in warmth—unfolding through everyday moments, spontaneous conversations, and unguarded laughter.

Sudheer admired her deeply. He often found himself wondering how someone could be so graceful, so rooted, and yet so light hearted. To him, Kamala was not just a part of the family—she was one of its most beautiful blessings. In her, he saw a rare combination of gentleness and resilience, of simplicity and emotional intelligence.

She found joy in the little things—in short, her motto was life is too short, so have to enjoy moment-. She celebrated life not with grandeur but with gratitude. To put in a nut shell, Sudheer learnt from her, the true Art of Living.

Sudheer cherished their bond and Kamala had been his steady thread of affection—someone who never forgot to include him, never stopped caring even from a distance. That night, the Bhai Dooj *diya* burned steadily despite the breeze—its flame steady, like the quiet heartbeat of an unspoken bond. For Sudheer, it wasn't just a ritual. It was poetry. A soft echo of a thousand sisterly affections, folded into one sacred moment. Maya's gesture stirred something older, deeper—a memory that had once glowed just as warmly.

He had left her home that night with a heart full of contentment, holding onto a memory that would become a refuge in the years to now, as Maya offered him a similar gesture, Sudheer's soul stood still between the present and the past. The beach breeze, the diya, the silence—it all mirrored that unforgettable day with Kamala. Though life had drifted, seasons had changed, and distances had grown, the feeling remained. Pure. Intimate. Undiminished.

He knew now that sisterhood was not defined by blood alone. It was defined by *feeling*—by those rare souls who saw you, celebrated you, and stood by you in both laughter and silence.

And tonight, as the Bhai Dooj flame flickered beside Maya, Sudheer smiled faintly—his heart silently thanking Kamala for the love that had outlived distance, silence and time.

CHAPTER 15: SHADOWS BEHIND THE SMILE

After the surprise Bhai Dooj celebration, something shifted in their bond. They had crossed a quiet threshold—from neighbourly warmth into the kind of sibling affection that didn't need definitions. Maya's care was never loud, never overwhelming. It came in the form of gestures.

One such evening, as they sat on the open terrace watching the orange hues of sunset blend into the sea, Maya said softly, "You remind me of someone I lost long ago."

"A brother?" he asked gently.

She nodded, not looking at him. "Not by blood, but in soul. He was... someone who just understood me without trying. It's been years, but sometimes I feel like... the bond just slipped into a new form."

The words struck Sudheer in a way he couldn't explain. There was a familiarity in her sadness. That gentle grief, that quiet longing—it echoed something he himself had felt before.

Days passed, and subtle things began to stand out. One afternoon, while helping Maya clear her attic, Sudheer noticed an old diary in stack of books. Out of habit, he flipped through a few pages. His fingers stopped at a handwritten poem—one he had penned decades ago and mailed to Kavitha Akka during his college years. It was a silly, emotional piece titled *"O My Sister of Letters"*—nothing famous, never published, something he thought had vanished into time.

He looked up, stunned. "Maya... how do you have this?" She paused, as if weighing memories and words. Then she smiled faintly, her eyes not quite meeting his. "I collect poems... especially ones that speak to the heart," she said. And then she closed the diary and moved on to the next shelf.

The explanation should've satisfied him—but it didn't.

That night, Sudheer sat on his bed staring at his old cassette player, playing Lata's "Yaara Seeli Seeli" on loop. Memories of Akka, those handwritten letters, the Sunday radio shows, and the lazy afternoons came flooding back. Maya's presence didn't replace any of that—but it somehow stirred it, deepened it, made him question whether life sometimes circled back in forms the heart recognized before the mind did.

All he knew was that his life had once again been touched by a woman who treated him not as an acquaintance or guest, but as a brother.

And yet, something about Maya's silences—about her familiarity with his past, her phrasing, her knowing smile—left a whisper of mystery in his otherwise simple, emotional world.

A whisper that would soon grow louder.

CHAPTER 16: ECHOES BETWEEN PAGES

A week had gone by since that Bhai Dooj evening, but its warmth still stayed with Sudheer. Every evening after work, he found himself walking along the beach. He'd stand there quietly, watching the waves come and go, feeling like the sea was talking to him in its own calm way. It was more than just nature now—it felt like a connection to his past and present, all rolled into one.

As his paying guest room was just across the road, facing the beach. Mornings were peaceful, and evenings even more so. Sometimes, he'd take a flask of lemon tea and sit on the terrace, letting the ocean breeze play with his hair while he lost himself in thoughts.

One evening, while he was sitting on the porch of Maya's house, she came out holding a small bundle wrapped in cloth. She looked a little shy, but her smile was warm.

"I want to show you something," she said. "I used to write a lot… letters I never sent, poems I never shared. Maybe you'll find something familiar in them."

Sudheer was surprised but took the bundle gently. It was an old diary—the kind that had seen time. Its pages were yellow at the edges, but it carried a soft scent of old paper and memories.

As he started flipping through the pages, he saw simple thoughts at first—notes about sunsets, being alone, and finding peace in silence. But then something stopped him. "You were never far. Just folded somewhere between a song and a letter. I see you in sunsets and smell you in lemon tea. I hear you in silence."

His heart skipped a beat.

These words reminded him of something from long ago. Kavitha Akka had once written something similar when he was posted away from home for the first time:

"Sudheer, you are never far from me. I hear you in the silence of our paused cassettes, smell you in the steam of lemon tea Amma makes. You live in the unsent letters I still keep writing."

He blinked, feeling a strange chill. It was like reading Akka's words again—but from someone else's pen.
He turned more pages.

"Waves fall. They rise again. So do we."

That line too—Akka had written it after his surgery years ago, when he had been at his lowest. She had told him:

"You may feel low now, but don't forget the ocean. The waves fall. They crash. But they always rise. You will too. You always have."

He closed the diary and stared at the sea beyond Maya's balcony. It wasn't confusion he felt—it was comfort. As if somehow, life had sent him another sister—not to replace Akka, but to remind him that love doesn't vanish. It changes shape, and sometimes, it returns through unexpected people.

He looked up and said

I used to get letters like this… from my Akka, Kavitha. They meant the world to me. And now... it feels like some of them are coming back through you."

Maya didn't respond. She just gave him a quiet smile. The sea wind blew gently. Somewhere nearby, a song floated on the air…

Ajnabee kaun ho tum...
Jab se tumhe dekha hai...
Saari duniya meri aankhon mein simat aayi hai...

That night, as Sudheer walked home, he looked up at the sky. The stars, the sea, and the silence—they all felt connected. Something inside him had changed. A feeling, a memory, a thread between then and now.

He realized: A letter written with love may take years… but it always finds its way back.

CHAPTER 17: THREADS FROM A FORGOTTEN LOOM

It was a quiet Sunday morning when Maya invited Sudheer for breakfast. The air was filled with the comforting aromas of ajwain parathas, paneer curry, and lemon tea. As they sat across the small table on the balcony overlooking the beach, Sudheer felt a calmness he hadn't known in a long time.

After a while, Maya returned with an old photo frame, slightly chipped at the corners. She placed it gently on the table between them. It held a picture of a boy—probably around ten years old—beaming with mischief.

“This is Karthik,” she said, her voice dipping with a softness that could only come from memory. “My little brother.”

Sudheer looked up slowly.

“He would have been your age now,” she continued, a distant smile on her lips. “He loved the sea too. Every evening, we’d come to this very beach. He used to say the waves listened better than people did.”

“What happened to him?” Sudheer asked, gently.

Maya took a deep breath. "When he was twelve, he fell seriously ill. It was sudden, something congenital we never knew about. He was gone within weeks. Just like that."

Sudheer's heart sank. The grief in her voice wasn't dramatic—it was quiet, but it lingered in the air like an unfinished lullaby.

"I stopped visiting the beach after that," Maya continued. "For years. I buried everything. His books, his toys… even the letters he used to write me when I went to college. I couldn't bring myself to read them."

Sudheer reached for the photo frame, his thumb brushing against the glass. "And now?"

"Now…" she smiled, meeting his eyes, "now I visit again. Ever since you came here. It felt… I don't know, like something had returned. Not exactly him, no. But the comfort, the rhythm, the feeling of being an elder sister again."

Sudheer felt a lump rise in his throat. There were no perfect words for such moments—only presence.

Later that evening, as the sun dipped below the horizon, they walked silently by the shore. The waves rolled in and out, constant, reassuring. Sudheer paused to write something in the wet sand:

Some bonds never fade. They just find new names.

Maya smiled when she saw it. “I think Karthik would have liked you,” she said softly

“And I think Akka would have liked you,” Sudheer replied.

They walked on, the wind scattering the writing in the sand—but not from their hearts

CHAPTER 18: THE UNHEARD VOICE

Evenings in Vizag had begun to feel emptier.

The golden light that once filtered through the window now fell on cold, quiet walls. Maya was gone—not forever perhaps, but gone from this chapter. There were no more unplanned beach strolls, no more silent smiles over lemon tea. Only memories... rich, vivid, aching memories.

Their bond, though brief and unspoken at times, had woven itself into Sudheer's heart like a delicate thread. Some relationships don't stay forever, but they don't vanish either; they leave marks, soft impressions that shape the soul's landscape. Maya's presence was like a fleeting melody—transient, haunting, beautiful—and though she had gone, the echo of her song lingered, reminding Sudheer that even the most temporary connections can transform us deeply.

Sudheer sat at his desk, the same old writing table where he'd once scribbled letters to Kavitha Akka years ago. Now, he opened a fresh sheet of paper, and began writing—not with the intention of sending it, but simply to let his soul breathe.

"Dear Akka... I don't know if you'll ever read this. But tonight, I'm filled with thoughts I can't hold inside. Maya walked into my life when I was least expecting it—and left before I was ready. She reminded me of everything I had once loved, everything I thought was lost in time. But she was never mine to keep. Just a diya in the silence—bright for a moment, then gone.

But Akka, why did her words feel so familiar? Why did her tears echo mine?

I don't know what Maya was running from, or what part of her past I was unknowingly reliving.

Was I her brother in a forgotten memory? Or was she the sister I once lost?

Maybe some bonds come back in different forms..."

He paused. His hands trembled slightly as he folded the letter and placed it into a small box—the same one where he stored every letter he'd ever received from Kavitha Akka.

Just as he tried to close the box, something unusual caught his eye. A folded piece of old paper tucked beneath the false bottom of the box. His breath stilled.

He pulled it out. It was yellowed with age, but untouched. The handwriting...

It looked just like **his own.**

"To Sudheer...

If you're reading this, you've met her. The one who reminds you of silence, of skies, of smiles that felt too familiar. Don't ask how or why. Some truths come to us before memories do.

You'll know what to do when it's time. Just remember... some letters are written with the soul, not the hand."
He reread it in disbelief. He didn't remember writing this. The paper smelled faintly of sandalwood. The words felt alive.

Was this something he wrote during a dark, forgotten phase? Was someone else playing with his memory? Or... was this something else altogether?

Sudheer placed both letters gently back into the box.
And that night, under a starlit sky, he whispered to himself—not with fear, but with quiet wonder:

"Some memories aren't made... they're remembered."

A few days after finding the mysterious letter, Sudheer visits an old bookstore near the beach, hoping for a distraction. The elderly owner, recognizing him from a past visit with Maya, hands him a journal she once left behind.

"She said she'd return for it... but never did. Maybe it's meant for you now."

At home, Sudheer flips through it and finds a loose, handmade sheet—an unsent, undated letter. No name. Yet it reads like Maya writing to a lost brother. As he reads, something stirs in him. The words feel... personal.

Excerpt from the Letter:

"To the one I never got to protect...
I searched for you in strangers, in silences.
Maybe we met, and I didn't know.
If we meet again, I won't ask your name. I'll just listen to your silence. And I'll know."
Sudheer reads it over and over.
Was this about him?
He recalls Maya's tears at the beach, her words: *"Some bonds don't begin. They just return."*
Was he a shadow of someone she lost?
Or were they both unfinished stories, briefly sharing a page?
He doesn't find the answers. But perhaps that's the point.
Closing the letter, he whispers,
"You did find him, Maya. Just not the way you expected."

CHAPTER 19: WAVES AND WHISPERS

The days passed like waves—sometimes crashing with memories, sometimes receding in silence. Sudheer no longer searched for answers. He had learned to live with the questions.

Yet one quiet morning, after months of reflection, he returned to the same beach where Maya and he once sat under the orange sky. This time, he wasn't here just to reminisce. He had a purpose.

A little wooden **bookstore**, newly opened, stood right where the sand kissed the land. Modest, with bamboo shelves and seashell wind chimes that danced with the breeze. A hand-painted board hung outside:

"Letters & Waves" – A Place for Stories and Goodbyes

It was his.

Sudheer had fulfilled a quiet dream: to open a space where people could read, write, and leave behind a piece of their heart.

There was a special section called ***"Unsent Letters"***, where anyone could drop a letter never meant to be posted. A box of emotions in paper form.

Some wrote to their lost ones, some to lovers who never knew, some to the versions of themselves they once were.

And tucked away behind the counter, beneath the cashbox, Sudheer kept **three letters**:

- One to Kavitha Akka.
- One that had mysteriously appeared in his own handwriting.
- And Maya's silent message to the brother she never named.

They say books tell stories. But some books are stories—**of lives, of love, of loss, of letters** never sent.

People who visited *Letters & Waves* often wondered about its name.

Some thought it was poetic.
Some thought it was nostalgic.

But Sudheer knew—it was about people. The ones who arrived like letters in his life. The ones who left waves in his heart.

And above all, it was about his sisters.

CHAPTER 20:

BACK TO THE BEGINNING, WHERE THE HEART STILL WRITES

That evening, the sea breeze slipped gently through the window as Sudheer turned the bookstore sign to “Closed ”. The sky had turned a pale lavender, and silence wrapped itself around the shelves like an old friend.

Just as he moved to shut the door, he noticed an envelope lying just beneath it—simple, cream-colored, with no stamp or name. Only a single line across the front:

"To the one who still writes with his heart."

No surprise crossed his face. Only a quiet pause.

He sat down at the small wooden desk near the window, opened the envelope, and began to read.

The Letter

Dear Sudheer,

You don’t know me, and that’s alright.

But I’ve visited your bookstore more than once—not just to read, but to feel.

The shelf titled *"For Her."* The unsent letters. The way you linger around memories without words…
It all reminded me of something precious I once lost.
Or maybe, something I never had.

I may be a stranger to you, but to me—you felt like a younger brother.

I watched quietly. And I understood.
So today, I'm doing something this fast world rarely does anymore—

I'm writing a letter.

I don't know who your *Akka* was, or what you still carry in silence.

But if you allow, let this be a small offering...
From one Akka,

To a brother I didn't expect to find in the quiet corner of a bookstore.

No expectations. No names to bind.

Just affection, wrapped in ink.

With warmth,
Anjali Akka

Sudheer folded the letter carefully, like a memory rediscovered.

He walked to the drawer where his most cherished letters lived—beginning with the one from Kavitha Akka. He placed Anjali Akka's beside it, not as a replacement, but as a quiet continuation of a bond that could never truly break.

This time, though, something felt different.

On the back of the envelope was a return address. No phone number. No email. Just an old-world thread, inviting him to respond the only way he knew how—through words from the heart.

Sudheer reached for his old writing journal.

And once again…
He began to write.

Later that evening, he placed that journal on the wooden stand near the entrance of the bookstore.

The sea breeze turned its pages softly, as if it wanted to read it first.

Sudheer stood silently, hand over his heart.

He didn't need closure.
He had **connection**.

And in a world full of noise, someone still saw him as a brother.

There was no greater honour... than to love someone as a sister.

Even if he stood alone now...
He was never truly alone.

Just then, as if the universe responded, his old Vividh Bharati radio app came to life with song playing….

"Ajeeb dastan hai yeh...
Kahan shuru, kahan khatam... Yeh manzile hai kaunsi
Na voh samajh sake na hum... "

The tune swayed through the air like a soft farewell—or maybe a promise.

He closed his eyes for a moment.

Then, without a word, he picked up a pen and opened a blank journal kept on the side table. On its dedication page, he wrote:

To every sister—real, lost, found, remembered.
You made my life a story worth telling.
If anyone ever reads this, know:
There is no greater comfort than knowing someone sees you as a brother.
And no greater honor than loving someone as a sister.

"Some stories don't end... they simply begin again in quieter ways."
Some bonds don't fade with time—
they simply change form, waiting to be felt again.

Sisterly Bond — The Heart of Sudheer

"Sudheer's world is shaped by the quiet strength of sisterly love a love that guides his instincts, colours his memories, and whispers in the gentle rhythms of his everyday life.

It is in the way he listens without words, cherishes without possession, and carries with him the unseen threads of every sister who touched his soul. This love is his compass and his solace the unseen force that turns tides and writes stories."

The love between a brother and sister is one of the deepest and noblest of human emotions.
It is not loud, not showy. But it is eternal.
It survives time, loss, silence, and even death.
It lives in memories, in letters, in sudden smiles, and unsaid prayers.
It was that love which shaped him.
It was that love which built this story.